Carter & Eli's Map Quest
Along the Turquoise Shores

By Kimberly Thornton
Illustrated by Viktoriia Davydova

Copyright © 2022. Kimberly Thornton. All rights reserved. No part of this publication may be reproduced, distributed, or transmitted in any form or by any means, including photocopying, recording, or other electronic or mechanical methods, without the prior written permission of the author, except in the case of brief quotations embodied in critical reviews and certain other noncommercial uses permitted by copyright law. For permission requests, write to the author, via website address below.

ISBN: 978-1-7774470-6-9 (Paperback)
ISBN: 978-1-7774470-7-6 (eBook)

Portions of this book are works of fiction. Any references to historical events, real people, or real places are used fictitiously. Other names, characters, places and events are products of the author's imagination, and any resemblances to actual events or places or persons, living or dead, is entirely coincidental.

Published by Kimberly Thornton, in Canada.

Second printing edition 2022.

Contact requests via website at: www.kimberlythornton.ca

Follow the real life adventures of Carter and Eli at animalsabroad.com

To my parents for supporting my dream with enthusiasm and encouragement.

Books in the Carter & Eli series...

1) Beyond the Icy Towers
2) Along the Turquoise Shores
3) Into the Golden Light

Table of Contents

Chapter 1:	Smooth Sailing	7
Chapter 2:	The Hidden World	13
Chapter 3:	Mysterious Stranger	23
Chapter 4:	Surprise Discovery	30
Chapter 5:	Persuasive Plan	39
Chapter 6:	A Roman Palace	45
Chapter 7:	Towering Heights	53
Chapter 8:	Stormy Seas	61
Chapter 9:	Fragrant Fields	71
Chapter 10:	Swarm Enemy	78
Chapter 11:	Perfect Stitch	86
Chapter 12:	The Canyon	92
Chapter 13:	On the Count of Three	100
Chapter 14:	Follow a Friend	105
Chapter 15:	The Missing Map	112
Chapter 16:	Daring Deception	120
Chapter 17:	The Next Adventure	131

Chapter 1
Smooth Sailing

"Eli, pull on the halyard," Eli's dad, Will, called from the deck of the boat.

Eli pulled as hard as he could on the rope attached to the head of the main sail. The large blue sail began to rise up the mast into the sky. Will turned the tiller to steer the sailboat to the right. As the boat shifted, the sail caught the wind and stiffened.

"Great job Eli," his mom, Hannah, said.

As they sailed out of the harbor, Eli looked

to the front of the sailboat, where his mom and little brother, Carter, sat enjoying the ride. Gazing up at the cloudless blue sky, Eli took

in the warmth of the sun and enjoyed the salty spray from the sea on his face. His dark brown hair blew in the breeze. It was a perfect day for sailing.

The Hayes family included ten-year-old Eli, seven-year-old Carter, and their parents, Hannah and Will. The whole family enjoyed travelling and adventure, so they recently left their home in Canada to go on a family trip around the world.

From the boat, Carter and Eli could see Naxos island, where they had been staying the last few weeks. Surrounded by the Aegean Sea, Naxos island is the largest of the Cyclades, a group of islands off the coast of Greece. Multiple shades of blue water surrounded the sandy beaches, and bright white buildings lined the shores and climbed up a mountainside. At the entrance to the harbour was a long footpath out to a smaller island.

As they floated out of the harbour, Eli called out, "What's that?" pointing to an enormous white marble frame sitting on the islet.

"That's the Portara, the temple of Apollo. It is the most famous monument in Naxos," his mother replied. "The frame is the entrance of what was supposed to be a grand temple for an ancient Greek ruler. Unfortunately, the temple was never completed because the ruler was overthrown before it could be finished. This is all that remains."

Carter and Eli looked at each other with excitement, imagining a fierce battle between ancient Greeks thousands of years ago. They wondered what it must have been like to live back then, during a time of mythical gods and powerful rulers.

"Shall we see how fast this boat can go?" Will asked, bringing them back from their thoughts.

Their dad had been teaching the boys to sail since they arrived in Naxos. Both Carter and Eli loved being out on the water and enjoyed the feeling of sailing.

"Can I let out the jib?" Carter asked, referring to the smaller sail at the front or bow of the boat.

"Sure. Do you remember how to do it?" his dad asked, shouting over the blowing wind.

"Yeah, I did it yesterday," he replied.

Carter waited for his dad to turn the sailboat into the wind. Then, when the main sail was slack, Carter pulled hard on the halyard attached to the jib's head. The smaller white sail shot up quickly and caught the wind. The boat gained speed, and they were out in open waters before they knew it.

Chapter 2
The Hidden World

Carter and Eli jumped off the boat onto the dock. They grabbed the ropes and tied up the bow and stern. Then, with the last knot pulled tight, they took off running. They headed down the dock to the beach, leaving Hannah and Will in the boat.

"Ouch, Ouch, Ouch!" Carter screamed. "My feet are burning."

"Quick, Carter, jump!" Eli called back to his little brother as he dove off the dock into the

clear water.

Carter followed, taking a running leap and curling himself into a cannonball position.

SPLASH!

Carter looked up to see his parents dripping wet. When he hit the water, the huge splash soaked Hannah and Will on the side of the dock.

Hannah wiped the water from her face. "You two have to wear your sandals. The dock is too hot to walk on."

"Yeah, we know, but this is way more fun," Carter giggled, floating on the water's surface.

With sandy blond hair, a friendly smile, and freckles sprinkled across his cheeks and nose, Carter had a playful look that matched his personality. He was adventurous and loved being around people and animals. You could often hear him sharing his animal facts with others.

Hannah and Will looked down at their wet clothes and laughed.

"Alright then," their dad said, rummaging

through his bag for a towel to dry off. "Meet us at the beach."

The boys took their time swimming to shore, enjoying the cool feeling of the water on their skin and spotting fish along the way.

"There's an orange one," Eli said, pointing to a small tropical fish circling them.

Eli was a quiet and thoughtful boy with a goofy and imaginative side that made him fun to be around. He was naturally curious and loved learning about new places, reading maps, and solving puzzles, especially ones involving math.

When they reached the shore, the boys stepped out onto powder-like sand.

"I'm starving," Eli called over to his parents, who had just reached the end of the dock.

"I could go for some calamari," their dad said. "Sailing always builds up an appetite."

"Sounds good. Let's take a seat at the café over there," their mom replied, pointing to a small group of tables to their right.

The tables and chairs sat on the beach.

Carter loved scrunching his toes in the sand while waiting for their food. There were bright white tablecloths on each table and blue umbrellas to shade them from the sun and heat.

The Hayes family sat down and ordered all their favorites, pastries filled with spinach and cheese called spanakopita, calamari or fried squid, and pita bread with tzatziki sauce.

"That was the best day yet," Eli said, shoving a piece of calamari in his mouth. "We went so fast. Can we go again tomorrow?"

"Not tomorrow. We are going on a bike ride in the morning and then meeting some friends for a picnic," their mom replied.

They stuff themselves with delicious food while relaxing and enjoying the ocean view.

The Hayes family loved the outdoors, especially being close to the water. It reminded them of their home in Vancouver.

"We better head back," their mom said, noticing the sun beginning to set. "It's been a big day."

***

The apartment they were in overlooked the sea and had large balconies off the main room and both bedrooms. When they arrived home, Carter and Eli went to their bedroom and jumped on the bed.

Lying on his back, staring up at the ceiling, Carter exclaimed, "I love it here. The beaches, the sunshine, and especially the sailing."

"Me too, but we've been in Greece for a while, and we still don't know which country we need to travel to next," Eli replied.

Before arriving in Greece, the Hayes family had visited Norway. While staying with relatives, Carter and Eli discovered an old letter addressed to their great-grandmother Liv. The letter described a mysterious treasure that could be found inside a Hidden World.

Many years ago, an ancient map to the Hidden World was torn into several pieces and scattered across the globe. If the treasure falls into the hands of the wrong person, it could result in disaster for all. Finding the letter meant they were chosen for a dangerous quest.

To discover the Hidden World, they would need to travel to many countries, solving riddles that would lead them to the missing map pieces.

While in Norway, the riddle took them on an adventure in the Arctic. The journey was dangerous, and they almost returned with nothing.

Eli joined Carter on the bed, holding the small wooden box they found during their first adventure. He used his index finger to trace over a symbol carved into the lid.

The symbol must have something to do with the Hidden World, thought Eli, but he couldn't figure out what.

He lifted the lid and took out the second riddle. Carter and Eli had read the clue many times and still couldn't figure it out.

You will find the country that you seek
Along the turquoise shore
Where colourful glass can be found
And an enchanted blue cave to explore.

"I still think it could be somewhere in Greece," Carter said.

"I know. There's definitely a lot of turquoise water here. But we haven't found anything about a blue cave," Eli replied.

"I know. It's tricky," Carter said with frustration. "Let's look at the second part of the riddle again. Maybe that will give us some more clues."

Eli flipped the paper over so they could see the writing.

Start where ancient civilizations collide
Past the island that moves with the tide
Pick a fragrant field, for protection it provides
Stop at the farthest rock as you have arrived
Cross the rocky terrain and then take a dive
Hold your breath and follow a friend inside.

During their adventure in Norway, they learned that each riddle had two parts. Solving the first riddle would tell them which country to travel to, and the second gave them clues leading them to the missing map piece.

Eli took the paper and put it back into the treasure box that held the first map piece.

"Maybe we can find a library on the island. Then we could do some research," he suggested.

"Mom said we're going on a bike ride tomorrow. Let's look for libraries as we ride," Carter replied.

"Good idea," Eli said, hiding the box at the bottom of his blue backpack.

Chapter 3
Mysterious Stranger

The sun was shining through the window when Carter woke up. He jumped out of bed and headed downstairs. He was usually the first one up in the morning, but when he entered the kitchen, his mom was already there.

"Morning love, how did you sleep?" she asked.

"Pretty good," he replied, grabbing a bowl from the cupboard. "Do we have any yogurt, Mom?"

"Yes, I just made myself a bowl with fruit. Do you want some help?" she offered.

"I'm okay."

Hannah took her tea and breakfast outside and sat at the balcony table to eat. Carter followed and sat down beside her. "Are we going to stay in Greece for much longer?"

"You know, your dad and I were just talking about that last night. We were thinking that we would like to move on to our next stop, but we can't decide where to go," she explained. "What do you think?"

"I really love it here, but I like to see new places, too," Carter replied.

He started to feel a bit worried. *What if the map piece was in Greece, and they left before finding it?* He asked himself.

"BOO!"

"Ahh!" Hannah screamed, clutching her chest in fear. She looked down to see Eli on the floor laughing. He loved to scare his mom.

"Eli! You got me again," she said, standing up and kissing the top of his head. "You two finish breakfast and get ready for the bike ride. We're going to leave soon."

"Okay, Mom," the boys said together.

"Eli," Carter said, trying to get his brother's attention, who was still on the floor laughing.

"ELI!" Carter yelled.

Eli stopped laughing. "What?"

"Listen, this is important. Mom and Dad are thinking about leaving Greece," Carter explained.

Eli was stunned. "No, we haven't figured out the next country yet."

Carter gathered his dishes. "I know. We are running out of time."

"Okay, we need to watch out for clues today," Eli said with urgency.

***

Carter and Eli were excited about the picnic. They couldn't wait to see their friends Ana and Mia. They pedalled their bikes around the winding streets, searching the many shops and buildings for a library, but there was none to be seen.

As they neared the park, their dad turned back to Hannah and the boys and asked, "Can we stop in here for a minute?"

He slowed down and moved to the side of the road. They were standing next to a tour operator store.

"I've heard there is some good diving around here, and I want to learn more about it," Will said. Their mom and dad loved to snorkel and scuba dive.

The Hayes family hopped off their bikes and went inside. The boys walked around the store while their parents were busy talking with the owner. To the left was a huge television showing a video of a diving trip. Carter was fascinated by the beautiful fish and sea plants.

"Carter," Eli called from the other side of the room. "Come over here."

Eli was standing in front of a long display case full of brochures about different tours. There was information on biking tours, boating trips, and scuba diving.

"I think I found something," Eli said,

picking up a brochure with an underwater cave. He handed it to Carter.

"Oh, wow! This cave is amazing. There are so many fish," Carter said, flipping through the colourful pages, "but it's not exactly blue."

"You know, if you two are interested in caves, you should go to Croatia."

Startled by the voice, the boys turned around to see a tall, slender man with broad shoulders. The man reminded them of a grandpa and wore light-colored pants with a button-down shirt. Over his arm, he had a suit jacket and hat. Staring at him, the boys thought it was much too hot to wear dress clothes.

"There is a lot of wildlife to see around Naxos, but Croatia has some of the most beautiful underwater caves in the world. There are even old shipwrecks that you can explore," the man continued.

Just as the boys were about to ask him more about the caves, their dad came up from behind. "Okay, guys, let's get going. We don't want to be late to meet Ana and Mia."

Carter and Eli turned back from their dad to the man in the suit. He was gone. They looked around, searching for him in the store, but it was as if he had vanished.

Chapter 4
Surprise Discovery

"Pass the ball, Eli," Carter yelled across the grassy field.

Eli kicked the soccer ball to his little brother. Carter steadied the ball before he ran toward the goal. He faked left, went around Ana, and took a shot. Mia lunged to the left corner of the goal and stopped the ball with her hands.

"Great, save Mia," Ana called to her older sister.

Ana and Mia Horvat were two of Carter and

Eli's favorite friends and among the best soccer players, they knew. Ana was seven years old, and Mia was ten, just like Carter and Eli. They had known each other for as long as they could remember. Their dads went to school together many years ago and remained good friends. It was always a special treat when they could spend time with them.

Carter noticed his mom coming over to them. "You guys must be hungry. Come over to the blanket and have some lunch."

The kids ran to the picnic area and sat down to eat, where a basket full of sandwiches and summer fruit sat under the shade of a large olive tree.

"How has your summer been so far?" Eli asked.

"Oh, it's been wonderful," replied Mia. "We spent the last month travelling in Croatia."

Eli turned to Carter and then looked back to the girls. That was the second time today that someone had mentioned Croatia to them.

Eli thought about the riddle again.

You will find the country that you seek
Along the turquoise shore
Where colourful glass can be found
And an enchanted blue cave to explore.

"Did you see a blue cave while you were there?" he asked.

"A blue cave?" Ana puzzled. "No, but we did go to Plitvice National Park. There were turquoise lakes surrounded by a huge forest. We went on a boat ride and saw many beautiful waterfalls. There were a few caves, but none were blue."

"My favorite was the Sea Organ in Zadar," Mia said excitedly.

"What's a Sea Organ?" Eli asked.

Mia stood up and explained, "Along the shore, in Zadar, there is a set of concrete steps that lead to the sea. Organ pipes were built into the steps. When the waves come in, they push and pull air in and out of the pipes, creating music. The different lengths of the organ pipes produce different notes, so it sounds like the sea is playing a song. That's why it's called the Sea Organ."

"Wow, that sounds neat," Eli replied. "What else did you do?"

"We visited with our grandparents mostly.

Our dad grew up in Croatia, and a lot of his family still lives there," Ana replied. "They live in a city called Split. It's so beautiful. The city is right on the water, and there are many interesting shops. Our grandpa has his own shop where he makes art out of glass. He's a glass blower."

Carter leaned closer to Ana and Mia, curious about their time in Croatia. "How does he blow glass?"

"First, he melts glass in a big fire pit, and then he takes one end of a long pipe and rolls the pipe in the melted glass. The hot glass sticks to the end of the pipe," Mia explained. "After that, he puts the other end of the pipe in his mouth and gently blows while turning it. The glass expands into different shapes, creating colourful ornaments."

The boys glanced at each other again, and Carter whispered, "Where colourful glass can be found."

"What did you say?" Ana asked.

"Nothing!" Carter and Eli said together.

"It's fascinating to watch," Ana added. "Our grandpa even took us to a museum with ancient glass made during the Roman Empire."

"I would really like to see glass blowing one day," Carter smiled.

After lunch, all four kids played another game of soccer. This time it was Mia and Carter versus Ana and Eli. They all had fun and were sad to see the day end. They said their goodbyes, and the Hayes family returned to their bikes and headed home.

"Mom, can we go to the beach for a bit?" Carter asked.

"Sure, but don't stay too late," Hannah replied. "Eli, keep track of the time and be home for dinner."

Eli looked at his navy blue watch. His parents had given it to him just before they left on their world trip. The watch face had numbers and letters, so it could be used to tell time and as a compass. The compass had proven helpful during their last adventure.

"No problem, Mom," Eli said.

Carter and Eli sat down at the water's edge, stretching their legs out so their feet could feel the waves as they came in.

"Do you think the next clue is in Croatia?" Carter asked.

"It sounds like it could be, but we still need to figure out the part about the cave. Mia and Ana didn't know anything about a blue cave," Eli replied.

"Why don't we ride back to the tour shop and see if there are any brochures on Croatia. We might be able to find some more information," Carter suggested.

Eli checked his watch. He wasn't sure if they would have enough time to go to the shop and make it home for dinner. "We'll have to be quick to get back in time," Eli said.

The boys ran to their bikes and pedalled as fast as they could to the tour shop they had visited earlier in the morning.

When they arrived, the store was locked, and the lights were off.

"It must have just closed," Eli said.

Carter and Eli sat down on the sidewalk, holding their backpacks, feeling disappointed.

"How will we find out about the cave now?" Carter asked.

"I guess we can ride back tomorrow."

Just then, something shiny caught Eli's eye. He peered down at the side pocket of his backpack and realized there was a piece of paper sticking out. Eli bent over and pulled it out. "What's this?" he asked, and Carter looked toward him. "It looks like a brochure of some kind," Eli said, holding it up for Carter to see.

With jaws wide open in surprise, their eyes focused on the writing on the paper - *Croatia's Famous Blue Cave.*

"Where did you get that?" Carter asked.

"I don't know. I've never seen it before," he replied. "I just noticed something in the pocket of my bag."

"That's strange!" Carter said.

Eli opened the brochure, and the boys stared at the picture of the Blue Cave. It reminded them of something out of a mythical book.

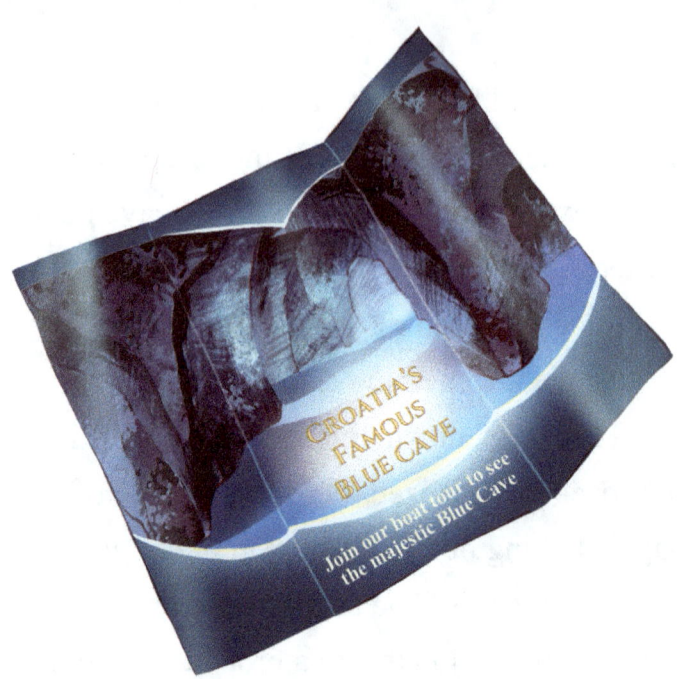

They smiled at each other, barely able to contain their excitement. They had solved the first part of the riddle. The next piece of the map was hidden somewhere in Croatia.

Chapter 5
Persuasive Plan

"How do you think that brochure got into your backpack, Eli?" Carter asked, walking their bikes into the garage of their apartment building.

Eli thought about it for a minute, going over the day's events. "I don't know. We looked around the store with Mom and Dad and then rode our bikes to the park to meet up with Ana and Mia. There wasn't anything unusual about it."

"Wait!" Carter cried. "What about the nice older man in the shop? He told us about Croatia having underwater caves."

"You don't think he put the brochure in my bag, do you?" Eli asked.

"It had to be him. No one else was there," Carter insisted. "But how did he know about the Blue Cave? Do you think he knows about the Hidden World?"

Before Eli could answer, the boys heard footsteps coming toward them.

"Shh," Eli whispered to Carter. He didn't want anyone to hear them talking about the Hidden World.

"There you guys are," Will said, coming around the corner. "I was just heading to the beach to look for you."

"Sorry, Dad, we lost track of time," Eli said.

"No problem, dinner is ready, so let's go before it gets cold," their dad said before walking up to the apartment.

Carter and Eli joined their parents at the dinner table on the balcony.

"Did you guys have fun today?" their mom asked, scooping pasta onto their plates.

"It was great," Eli said. "I love hanging out with Ana and Mia. They were telling us about their time in Croatia with their grandparents. It sounded amazing."

Excited, Carter could barely get the words out. "Yeah, they went to a place with a bunch of lakes and waterfalls, and the sea played music, and their grandpa showed them how to blow glass."

"Slow down, buddy," Will smiled. "It sounds great. I've always dreamt of travelling to Croatia. There is a lot of history and a beautiful coastline to explore."

"Yes, I've heard that Croatia is lovely. I would like to see the Sea Organ as well. Is that what you were talking about, Carter?" Hannah asked.

"Yes. Mia said that there are steps down to the sea, and when the waves hit them, it creates music," Carter explained.

"That would be such a unique experience. It

sounds wonderful," Hannah said.

Eli wiggled in his seat, trying to pull the Blue Cave brochure out of his pocket. When he managed to free it, he held it out. "Dad, Carter and I found this at the shop today."

Will gazed at the colourful pictures. "It's like magic," their dad exclaimed. "The whole cave shimmers." He turned the pamphlet over. "The brochure says that 'when the sunlight hits the cave just right, the inside turns blue, and the objects in the water become a sparkling silver colour.'"

Eli winked at Carter, realizing their plan was working. Their parents seemed interested in Croatia. Now they just had to convince them to go.

"Can we go to Croatia next?" Carter asked. "Mom, you said that you and Dad were thinking it was time to move on to our next stop, so why not Croatia?"

"Yeah, Dad. You love diving, and you promised that we would do some more snorkeling. So it's perfect," Eli added.

Will chuckled. "I think they've made up our minds," he said, and Hannah laughed.

"Well, I guess we should get packing," Hannah agreed, and Carter and Eli let out a huge cheer.

Chapter 6
A Roman Palace

The plane touched down in Split, Croatia, and Carter and Eli jumped in their seats to get off and explore.

Split, one of the larger cities in Croatia, sits on a peninsula that juts out into the Adriatic Sea. Off the coast of Split are several islands surrounded by turquoise water.

The Hayes family stepped out of the airport and breathed in the warm salty sea air. They gathered their bags and jumped on a bus that would bring them to where they would stay while in Croatia. Carter and Eli felt lucky because they would stay with Ana and Mia's grandparents. Carter couldn't wait to see how to blow glass and secretly hoped that Mr. Horvat would let him try.

The bus slowed down in front of a two-story house in a busy part of town. People were everywhere, walking in the streets or enjoying an afternoon snack at one of the cafés. Cheerful music and the sounds of people laughing filled the air. The boys looked up and saw a beautiful archway covered with bright green leaves that led into a courtyard.

"Hello, my friends," an older man said, walking over to them.

He had dark hair with a bald spot on top and a bushy mustache. Behind his thin-framed glasses were brown eyes that squinted in the bright sunlight.

"Will, it's nice to see you again. I hope your travels went smoothly."

Will went over to shake hands with the older

gentleman. "Hello, Mr. Horvat. It's great to see you. It was a good trip, just a short flight from Greece to Croatia."

The older man walked over to Carter and Eli. "You must be Eli and Carter," he said. "Ana and Mia have told me so much about you. My name is Ivan. I'm their grandpa."

Just then, a young boy came running over. He was about Eli's age and had black hair that fell into his bright green eyes and a playful smile.

"Hi, I'm just about to head to the beach to swim. Do you want to come?"

Ivan laughed. "This is my grandson Luka, Mia and Ana's cousin. We can't keep him out of the water."

"Well, that makes three of them," Hannah said, looking over at Carter and Eli with a smile. "Why don't you go and play while we unpack," she suggested.

The three boys set off to the water, walking down a narrow street shaded by large trees. The boys noticed fruit stands, butcher shops, and bakeries scattered between apartments and houses as they walked.

"Let's stop over here," Luka suggested,

walking toward a small café.

The boys went inside and could instantly smell the sweet aroma of baked goods. At the counter, in front of them, was a large display case with an assortment of cakes and treats.

"The cherry strudel is the best," Luka said.

That sounded delicious to Carter and Eli, so they ordered three to take away. Once at the beach, they sat down on the sand to enjoy their treats.

"What do you like to do around here?" Eli asked.

"Oh, there's so much to do. I spend a lot of time swimming and sailing. My family has a small sailboat we keep docked at the main harbor. And I like to visit the Old Town," Luka replied.

"What's in the Old Town?" Carter asked.

Luka stood up to grab a rock and threw it into the sea. "A large part of the Old Town is formed by Diocletian's Palace. But it looks more like a fortress than a palace. Once you enter the main gate, you are walking around an ancient walled city. The alleyways are made of stone and lined with brick buildings. You will find many shops and restaurants inside," Luka explained. "Diocletian's Palace was built next to the Adriatic Sea, so many people often visit the Old Town."

Eli was curious at the mention of a palace. "Who is Diocletian?"

"Diocletian was a Roman emperor who built the palace in A.D. 305. He lived there with his family."

"Can we go inside the palace?" Carter asked.

"Yeah, there are a few areas that you can go and see," Luka replied. "I like to go to the Cathedral of Saint Domnius to see the huge black sphinx just outside. There's also a bell tower next to the cathedral that you can climb to the top of. From there, you can see all of Split."

"A sphinx?" Eli asked, confused. "I thought you said the palace was made by a Roman emperor. Why would a sphinx be there? Those are from ancient Egypt."

"An Egyptian pharaoh sent as many as twelve sphinxes as gifts to the emperor," Luka explained, "but only one remains intact."

"That's interesting. A palace made for a Roman emperor decorated with sphinxes from ancient Egypt," Eli said. Then he gasped, remembering the riddle. *Two ancient civilizations coming together in one place.* He thought.

Eli leaned over to Carter and whispered, "This must be where we begin! Start where ancient civilizations collide."

Carter's eyes lit up with surprise.

On their walk home, Carter and Eli decided to visit the palace as soon as possible. When they arrived at the apartment, they were tired from the day's events.

"Hi guys, did you have fun?" Hannah asked.

"It was great, Mom. We had cherry strudel and went swimming," Carter said excitedly.

"Luka also told us about a palace built more than a thousand years ago for a Roman emperor. So we thought we would go check it out," Eli explained.

"That sounds fun. Why don't you go tomorrow? Dad and I have to work," their mom suggested. "Mr. Horvat has two bikes you can borrow if you like."

"That sounds great," Eli said with a large yawn.

"It looks like you guys are ready for bed," their mom said as the boys shuffled to their room. "Goodnight, loves."

"Goodnight, Mom," Carter and Eli replied.

Chapter 7
Towering Heights

"Can you pass me my backpack?" Eli called to Carter, who was on the other side of their bedroom.

Carter grabbed Eli's blue backpack from the closet and threw it over to him on the bed.

"Mom made sandwiches and snacks to take with us, and I have emergency supplies. What else should we bring?" Carter asked.

"It's hard to say. We needed all sorts of stuff the last time," Eli replied, referring to their

Arctic adventure. "The riddle said we need to take a dive, so we're going to get wet. Let's bring our waterproof bag and flashlights."

"Good idea. We can put the riddle in the waterproof bag to keep it safe," Carter added, packing his orange backpack. "I can't wait to get going."

"Me too," Eli said, pulling the zipper shut on his bag. "I think we're ready."

Carter and Eli put on their backpacks and sandals and headed to the front door.

"Mom, Dad, we're leaving for the palace now," Eli called to their parents.

Hannah met them at the door. "Love you," she said, giving them each a hug. "Have fun and stay together."

***

It was a short ride from Mr. Horvat's house to Diocletian's Palace. They slowed down their bikes as they approached the Old Town. Just outside the walled city was a large courtyard with rows of tables full of fresh fruits, vegetables, and flowers.

They rode passed the market and stopped at the eastern gate of the white stone structure.

"Luka was right. It does look more like a fortress," Carter said.

"Imagine the battles that must have happened here," Eli wondered. "The walls are enormous. They must have been able to defend themselves from all directions."

Carter and Eli parked their bikes off to the side and walked through the open gate. Inside, the stone alleyways were full of shops and people.

"Let's look at the riddle," Eli said, taking off his backpack and bending down to open it. He pulled the old piece of paper out of the waterproof bag.

Start where ancient civilizations collide
Past the island that moves with the tide
Pick a fragrant field, for protection it provides
Stop at the farthest rock as you have arrived
Cross the rocky terrain and then take a dive
Hold your breath and follow a friend inside.

"We know we're in the right place, so there must be a way to see the island that moves with the tide from somewhere in the palace," Carter said, thinking out loud.

"What about the bell tower?" Eli suggested. "Luka said that you could see the whole town from up there. Maybe we'll be able to see the islands as well."

"There it is," Carter said, pointing to the left of the courtyard.

The boys took off, racing. The grand bell tower, the tallest structure in the palace, was easily seen from all areas of the Old Town.

Eli slowed as he reached the bell tower next to the Saint Domnius Cathedral. "There's the sphinx!"

A giant Egyptian sphinx sculpted out of black granite towered over them. Standing face to face with the mythical creature, Carter was in awe. "I hope to see the real Sphinx one day."

"That would be amazing," Eli agreed. He walked up a set of stairs leading to a large wooden door. "This must be the entrance to the bell tower. Let's go inside."

Eli suddenly stopped when he walked inside the bell tower. Frozen, he stood next to Carter and gasped. Archways and windows lined the walls of the tower, letting the sunlight in from outside. It was so bright. It was easy to see all the way to the top.

"Are you okay?" Carter asked.

"It's pretty high," Eli said nervously.

Eli had always been afraid of heights. Carter took his hand. "We'll go up together. Just don't look down."

Eli took a deep breath and walked toward the staircase. The boys held on to the narrow railing and started to climb.

The stairs seemed to float up the sides of the square tower, creating an open space in the middle. Eli counted the steps as they went up to distract himself from the height above the ground.

"Two hundred!" he shouted when they reached the last step and walked onto a landing.

From the top, they could see the entire town

of Split and the islands off the coast. Carter opened his backpack and took out a pair of binoculars.

"There are a lot of islands out there. Which one do you think it is?" Carter asked, scanning the shoreline.

Focused on figuring out the riddle, Eli didn't hear Carter's question. Instead, he wandered around the platform, searching for clues. There were a few signs with interesting facts about the bell tower and the town of Split. One sign, in particular, caught his eye. On it was a picture of a white beach surrounded by teal-blue water.

"Carter, come over here," Eli called to his little brother. "I think I found something."

Carter ran over to where Eli was standing next to the sign.

"The tip of Zlatni Rat beach changes direction depending on the wind and the currents," Eli explained. "It's the riddle. We have to go *past the island that moves with the tide.*"

"That's it! You found it, Eli. We need to go

past Brac island!" Carter yelled, jumping up and down with excitement.

"Now we just need to find a boat to get there."

"Luka said his family has a sailboat. Maybe he'll let us borrow it," Carter suggested.

Eli turned to Carter with a big smile. "Let's go find him."

Chapter 8
Stormy Seas

Carter and Eli found Luka at the main dock, washing his family's sailboat.

"Hi, Luka," Carter shouted, running down the dock.

"Hi guys, how's it going?" Luka replied.

"Good. We went to Diocletian's Palace today and climbed up the bell tower. We could see the whole town and the islands. Just like you said," Carter explained.

"That's great. I love it up at the top of the

tower," Luka agreed.

"The islands looked so nice, we thought we would try exploring them. Do you think we could borrow your sailboat?" Eli asked.

"Sure, you can use it," Luka replied. "I'm helping my grandpa at his shop this afternoon. Will you be okay to sail without me?"

"Yeah, we know how to sail. Our dad taught us while we were in Greece," Eli explained.

Luka looked up at the sky. "You may want to wait a bit. Those clouds look like they could bring some rain."

Carter and Eli gazed up. Dark grey clouds were coming in from the west, and the wind seemed to be picking up a bit.

"A little rain won't hurt us," Eli laughed.

"Alright," Luka replied. "Which island are you going to go to?"

"We're not sure yet," Carter replied.

"If you head south and steer through the channel, Brac island will be on your left, and just past it is Hvar island. They both have nice beaches and great swimming," Luka suggested.

"Thanks," Eli said. "We'll head that way."

"I have to go now, or I'll be late to meet my grandpa," Luka said, gathering his things and waving goodbye. "Have fun. I'll see you later."

"Bye, Luka. Say hi to your grandpa for us," Carter called after him.

When Luka was gone, Carter and Eli threw their bags into the sailboat. They jumped onto the deck, untied the ropes, and pushed off the dock. Eli used the compass on his watch to navigate south.

"Carter, go up to the bow and set up the jib. While you're doing that, I'll work on the main sail," Eli said.

The boys got to work organizing the sails. Carter went up to the front of the boat and grabbed the jib sheets, the ropes that control the smaller sail. Eli had just finished setting up the main sail when Carter rejoined him at the back of the boat.

"Ready?" Eli asked.

"Ready," Carter replied with a thumbs up. He couldn't wait to get on the water again.

Eli steered the boat out of the harbour. "Let out the sails," he called to Carter.

With full sails, the boat began to pick up speed and headed out to sea. The water was rough through the channel, but the boys enjoyed the bumps.

Eli noticed an island to his left. "Look, Carter, there's Brac island."

"We're on the right track," Carter said, excited to start their next adventure.

As they sailed farther out to sea, shadows fell over them. Carter and Eli could see angry clouds above. The sun was gone. They stared at each other nervously, realizing they were heading into a storm.

A flash of lightning pierced the sky, followed by the low rumble of thunder. Scared, Carter closed his eyes and covered his ears. Suddenly, pellets of rain began to fall, and the wind started to howl. Waves crashed against the side of the sailboat, pushing it side to side like a toy in a bathtub.

"Carter, grab hold of the ropes," Eli called.

"We have to keep control of the sails, or we could tip over."

Carter went to grab the rope for the jib, but it slipped out of his hand. The rope blew to the front of the boat and tangled around the mast.

"I'll get the rope. You steer the boat," Eli told Carter.

Eli crawled to the bow while Carter used the tiller to steady the boat. But the waves were now crashing up and over the side, flooding the deck.

Using one hand to balance and the other to cover his eyes from the salty splashes, Eli reached the front of the boat and grasped the mast. He freed the jib rope and tossed it back to Carter to secure it.

"Quick, come back," Carter shouted. "The waves are getting bigger. It's too dangerous to be up there."

Eli turned around to come back. Then a huge wave crashed into them just before he jumped onto the deck. Eli's feet slipped on the wet surface, and he fell. With his feet dangling

overboard, Eli held on to the side of the boat with all his strength.

"HELP!" Eli screamed. "I can't hold on much longer."

Carter rushed to Eli and grabbed his arms but struggled to pull him back into the boat. Eli was much bigger than him, and he didn't have the strength. Quickly, Carter thought of another plan. He grabbed a rope and tossed it over to Eli.

"Eli, grab the rope. I need you to help pull yourself up," Carter shouted.

Just as Eli took hold of the rope with his right hand, another large wave smashed into him, knocking him against the side of the boat. He tightened his grip, but it was no use. His fingers slipped through the rope.

Carter screamed, seeing his older brother hanging off the side, holding on to the boat with only one arm. He leaned over and reached for Eli's hand. The boat rocked back and forth, making it impossible for their hands to meet.

Finally, their fingers locked. "I got you," Carter shouted. "Grab the rope."

Eli gripped the rope and pulled himself up the side of the hull. Knowing this was his only chance to save his brother, Carter used all his strength to drag Eli back into the boat.

The boys fell backward and slammed into the deck. Then, ignoring the pain they felt from the fall, they stood up and took control of the boat.

"We have to get to land," Eli shouted over the loud whistling wind and cracking thunder. "Over there," he yelled. "There's a beach."

"We have to turn, or we'll miss it," Carter shouted.

Carter and Eli grabbed the ropes for the sails. Everything was slippery from the rain and the waves. It was hard to keep hold of the ropes and steady themselves in the rocking boat.

"On three," Eli said, and Carter nodded.

Eli turned the boat into the wind. "One, two, three, go!"

As soon as Eli let out the sail, the boys ducked. The boom swung across to the other side and caught the wind. The boat turned to the left, and they began heading toward the island. Carter and Eli fought to stay on course, battling against the fierce winds and strong currents.

After what felt like hours, the boat slammed into the sandy beach, knocking Carter and Eli to the floor.

They pulled themselves over the side of the

boat and collapsed on the ground. Then, lying face down, exhausted, and relieved to be back on land, Carter and Eli drifted off to sleep.

Chapter 9
Fragrant Fields

"Ahh!" Eli cried, rolling over onto his side.

Holding his stomach, he stood up. The sky was blue. There was no trace of the storm that had just occurred. Covering his eyes with his arm to block the bright sun, he looked around to see where they had landed.

"Ouch!" Carter called as he began to wake up.

"Are you okay? What hurts?" Eli asked Carter, walking toward him.

"My leg mostly," Carter replied. "I think I twisted it when we were trying to turn the boat. What about you?"

Eli pulled up his shirt and noticed a large purple bruise below his rib cage. "I'm okay, but my side hurts."

"That doesn't look good. Are you able to keep going?" Carter asked.

"Yeah, we have to. We have to find the next map piece and clue," Eli replied.

Eli helped Carter stand up. They brushed the white sand off their clothes and faces and turned to the boat.

"Is it damaged?" Carter asked.

"I'm not sure. Let's go check it out."

Carter followed Eli toward the sailboat, limping behind him. Eli noticed and came back to help him. He put his arm under Carter's armpit so Carter could lean on him while they walked.

Soon after the boys crawled back into the boat, they faced a disappointing discovery. The bright green main sail flapped in the wind, showing off a large tear in the centre.

"Oh no!" Carter shouted. "What are we going to do?"

"It's not too bad." Eli held up the damaged sail. "We'll have to sew it back together."

"I have a sewing needle in my Swiss Army knife," Carter said, pulling the shiny red object out of his pocket. It was a gift from his parents before they left on the world trip, and similar to Eli's watch, the many gadgets had come in handy on their last adventure.

"Great, now let's find some thread," Eli smiled.

The boys searched under the seats, inside the boat's cabin, and in every cupboard and drawer, they could find. There was no thread.

Finally, Eli rummaged through a small cabinet under the stairs. "I found a map," Eli called

"Let's see," Carter said, running up to his brother.

Eli spread the map out on the deck and knelt beside it. Carter crouched behind him.

"It's a map of all the islands. There's Split, and that's the channel we went through," Eli explained to Carter. "Based on this, I think we're on Hvar island just past Brac island. We can use the map to help us figure out where to go next."

"We're not going to go anywhere if we can't fix the sail," Carter reminded him.

"Right, let's keep looking," Eli replied.

The sun beat down on them as they searched the boat for some thread to fix the sail. Finally, with sweat rolling down the side of his face, Eli stopped. "I'm not sure we'll find anything we can use to fix the sail on the boat. Maybe we should see if we can walk into town and find a store."

"You're probably right," Carter agreed.

Eli checked his watch. It was already afternoon. "We have to hurry, or we won't be able to get home in time."

They left their backpacks and jumped out of the boat. Carter was still having some trouble with his leg but was able to walk with a limp.

"Are you sure you can come with me?" Eli asked.

"I'm not going to let you go alone."

"Alright, let me know if you need help," Eli offered as he walked away from the boat.

The sandy beach turned to a dirt path surrounded by grass and desert plants. Then, Eli noticed a familiar-looking plant. "Carter, there's an aloe plant."

Eli remembered seeing the plant when they went on a hike with their parents in California. His dad had shown him how to break it open and taught him that the sticky green gel inside could heal scratches, sunburns, and bug bites.

Carter broke off a leaf and rubbed the slimy substance between his fingers. "It feels cool to the touch."

The brownness of the desert was soon replaced by green as they walked farther away from the beach. Before long, the boys were standing in a grassy meadow. The smooth blades of grass tickled the back of their knees as they swayed in the breeze.

"Something smells nice," Carter noticed.

In the distance, the boys could see a field of purple. They hurried toward the flowers, curious to see what they had discovered.

"Lavender," Eli said. "It's a lavender field."

"*Pick a fragrant field, for protection it provides*," Carter whispered.

"What did you say?" Eli asked.

"I wonder if it could be the riddle," Carter replied. "We are supposed to pick something from a fragrant field that will protect us. Do you think it could be the lavender?"

"Maybe," Eli replied. "Let's take some, just in case."

"Sounds good," Carter agreed, picking some lavender flowers and putting them in his pocket. "What do you think we need protection from?"

"I have no idea, but based on our last adventure, it could be anything," Eli said, laughing and Carter joined in.

Just then, the boys heard feet shuffling in the dirt. They looked up. Their laughs caught in their throats, and fear spread across their faces.

Chapter 10
Swarm Enemy

"Seymour!" Eli grumbled through clenched teeth.

A sinister smile grew across Seymour's face. "Hi, buddy. Looks like you two are at it again."

Carter took a step back to be closer to Eli. Afraid of what Seymour might do.

"I'm not your buddy," Eli shouted, feeling his anger grow inside him, reminded of the betrayal he felt the last time they met.

Seymour appeared amused by the situation.

"Settle down, Eli. I'm just having some fun."

"You're not having fun. You're trying to steal our riddle," Carter screamed.

"You really need to be more careful. Just like the last time, it was easy to track you down."

Shocked, Carter gasped at Seymour. "You've been following us the whole time?"

Before he could respond, Eli glared at Seymour, refusing to take his eyes off him. "What do you want?"

"I think you know what I want," Seymour replied. "Hand over the riddle. This is my treasure to find. It's owed to me."

Seymour lunged at the boys trying to grab them. Carter and Eli jumped back, barely escaping his grasp.

"We'll never give it to you!" Carter yelled.

Eli grabbed a stick from the ground and approached Seymour, waving it toward his face. Seymour stepped back to avoid being hit, surprised the boys would fight back.

CRUNCH!

All three stopped, startled by the sharp sound. After a few seconds, a soft buzzing noise rose up in the air and surrounded them. Carter and Eli remained still as the humming grew louder and louder. Then suddenly, wasps began to fly up from the lavender plants. Panicked,

Seymour realized his boot had crushed a wasp's nest buried in the ground.

Swarms of angry wasps came rushing out, ready to defend their hive. They circled Seymour, stinging him over and over. He waved his arms, batting them away, but it only made the insects angrier. The frantic wasps flew in all directions and began to chase Carter and Eli.

Turning around, Eli yelled to Carter, "RUN!"

The boys ran as fast as they could back to the boat. Carter, with his injured leg, struggled to keep up. By the time they reached the dirt path, the wasps were closing in on them.

"Keep going, Carter. We're almost there," Eli called.

Carter tripped over a rock and crashed down, falling on his knees. "Ahh!" Carter wailed, tears streaming down his freckled cheeks.

Hearing the cries of pain, Eli rushed back to help him. But, the wasps had already surrounded Carter, stinging him. Eli pulled his little brother up and helped him to run.

Eli looked ahead and saw the beach. "Keep running until we get to the water. The wasps won't follow us in."

The boys dove into the sea and swam away from the shore. They sunk down, holding their breath until only the tops of their heads could be seen above the water. Soon, the wasps began to retreat, heading back to their hive.

Poking his head out of the water, Eli took a deep breath. "I think they're gone. Let's swim back to shore."

"I can't believe how many wasps there were," Eli said, climbing into the boat. "I wonder what happened to Seymour?"

Carter didn't respond. Huddled in the corner, Carter's blue eyes were red, puffy, and full of tears. Wasp stings covered his arms, and a deep cut spread across his knee from where he fell.

"Oh no, let me help you," Eli said, giving his little brother a hug. "I'll get some bandages."

"The stings hurt," Carter whimpered.

Unsure of what to do, Eli searched in his backpack to find something to take the pain away. There was nothing. Then he remembered the aloe plants they had seen.

Eli hopped out of the boat. "Stay here. I'm going to get some aloe. That should help."

Minutes later, Eli returned with a bunch of aloe leaves. He broke them in half and used his thumb and finger to push the sticky gel onto Carter's stings. "Does that feel better?"

"Yeah, it's starting to hurt less," Carter replied, rubbing his arms and legs. "What are we going to tell Mom and Dad? They'll never believe I got all these stings and hurt my leg at the palace. And you have a huge bruise on your side."

"Don't worry. We'll think of something," Eli said with a smile.

Chapter 11
Perfect Stitch

"Let's hurry and push the boat back in the water before Seymour finds us," Eli said, jumping onto the white sand.

"We haven't fixed the sail yet," Carter reminded him.

"I know, but it will be safer to float out in the water than to be on shore while we figure it out," Eli explained. "That way, Seymour won't be able to reach us."

Carter and Eli placed their hands on the

bow and used their strength to push the sailboat into the water. The strong current carried them away from the island. Once they were far enough offshore, Eli searched the boat again for something to mend the sail with. After a while, he sat back, feeling discouraged. "I don't think there's anything on this boat we can use to fix the sail."

"We can't give up," Carter urged. "Is there another way to get to the island? Maybe we can find a different boat," Carter suggested.

"Where are we going to find another boat? Plus, we have to bring this one back to Luka," Eli replied.

"I know, but we're so close," Carter whispered sadly.

Just then, a strong breeze caught the rope from the main sail. Eli lunged across the deck to grab it before it went overboard.

With the rope in his hand, his eyes widened with an idea. "Carter, we can use the rope to fix the sail."

"Isn't the rope too thick to go through the

needle?" Carter questioned.

"We can unravel the rope and use a small thread that will fit," Eli said, showing Carter how to loosen the rope.

Carter took out his Swiss Army knife, cut a small piece of rope, and began to take it apart. Once the rope was untangled, he handed the needle and thread to Eli. Then, sitting together on the edge of the boat, the boys lowered the main sail and sewed it back together.

"What do you think Seymour meant when he said that this was his treasure to find?" Carter asked. "He said it was owed to him. Don't you think that's strange?"

"Yeah, that was an odd thing to say." Eli paused from sewing. "I'm not sure what he meant, but he seems set on finding the treasure or stealing it from us. So we'll have to be more careful to make sure we're not being followed."

Carter nodded in agreement. Seymour scared him more than he wanted to admit.

"All done!" Eli said, holding the sail up to admire his work. "Hopefully, it will last until

we get back."

"You did it!" Carter cheered. "Now we can keep going." Then he hesitated a moment, tilted his head, and asked, "But where are we going?"

Carter pulled out the riddle from their waterproof bag.

Start where ancient civilizations collide
Past the island that moves with the tide
Pick a fragrant field, for protection it provides
Stop at the farthest rock as you have arrived
Cross the rocky terrain and then take a dive
Hold your breath and follow a friend inside.

"We found the palace and then sailed past Brac island. We collected lavender from Hvar, so now we need to go to *the farthest rock*," Carter said, reviewing the riddle.

"The clue must be referring to an island." Eli pulled out the map they had found earlier. "There's a small island here," he said, pointing to the map. "We have to continue southwest."

"Which island is it?" Carter asked.

"Bisevo."

"Wait, that's the island with the Blue Cave. Maybe the map piece is in there," Carter thought excitedly. "I really want to see that."

"Me too," Eli replied, setting their course on his compass. "We better hurry. Bisevo is far offshore. It will take a while to sail there."

Chapter 12
The Canyon

The salty breeze ruffled their hair as they sailed full speed toward the farthest rock. Soon they saw an island up ahead.

"There it is!" shouted Carter.

Eli checked the map. "I think that's Vis. Bisevo should be behind it. Let's sail around the island and check."

Carter and Eli adjusted the sails to change the direction of the boat. Once they passed Vis, a smaller piece of land came into view. Thrilled that they had arrived, the boys jumped up.

"There isn't anywhere to dock the boat," Carter realized. "We'll have to put the anchor down and swim to shore."

Eli unhooked the chain and dropped the anchor. Then he gathered their bags from under the seats. "Let's only take what we need so that it's easier to swim," he suggested.

"I'll get the waterproof bag," Carter said, pulling a smaller yellow bag from his backpack.

The boys packed the riddle and their waterproof flashlights and left everything else in the boat.

Carter stepped up to the stern of the boat and yelled, "Cannonball!"

Eli laughed at his little brother and jumped in after him. The shallow water was turquoise and as warm as a bath. They swam a short distance to a small cove on the island.

"Where to now?" Eli asked. "The riddle said we had to cross the rocky terrain and then take a dive."

"There's a path over there," Carter said,

pointing to a trail that went up a hillside.

They found themselves in a desert landscape when they reached the top of the hill. The sandy path was covered with small pebbles and lined with patches of dry grass. Beyond, they could see a vast copper-coloured rock formation.

"Which way should we go from here?"

"The path is rocky, so maybe we're on the right track. Let's follow it for now and see where it takes us," Carter suggested.

With the yellow bag around Eli's shoulder, they set off on the trail heading to the far side of the island.

After a while, the path narrowed between two rock faces. The opening was just big enough that the boys could fit through, walking side by side. They realized they were at the bottom of a large canyon. Inside, the canyon walls were jagged with small ledges that could be used to climb.

"Do you think we should keep walking or climb up?" Carter asked nervously.

"We don't have any climbing rope, so we'll

have to keep walking."

Slowly, Carter and Eli started down the narrow path. When they approached the centre, they heard a rustling sound from above. Something was moving on one of the rock ledges, but the glare from the sun prevented them from seeing what it was.

Standing frozen with fear, the boys waited for whatever was coming toward them.

Carter grabbed Eli's hand when he finally saw the creature that emerged. "Horned viper."

"What?" Eli asked, not able to hear Carter's whisper.

"That's a horned viper snake," Carter repeated.

More rustling came from above as dozens of giant snakes slithered their way down to the bottom of the canyon. They were brown with a diamond shape pattern on their back and a distinct horn on the tip of their nose. Eli turned his head from side to side. Snakes were blocking both ways out. They were trapped.

"Are they dangerous?" he asked.

"Yes," Carter replied with a shaky voice. "Their fangs have venom. One bite will kill you."

The snakes were right next to them now. Carter and Eli huddled close together, convinced they would not get out of this alive.

"What should we do?" Eli quivered.

Wishing he had a better plan, Carter hesitated, then muttered, "Stay very still and hope they leave."

Suddenly, a snake lunged at Carter. Its mouth was wide open, and its fangs dripped with venom. Then, just as the viper was about to strike, it stopped and slithered away.

Shocked by the snake's sudden retreat, Carter and Eli stared at each other confused. Carter put his hand next to his side and felt something hanging out of his pocket. He looked down and pulled it out.

"Eli, the lavender. Remember the riddle. *Pick a fragrant field, for protection it provides.* The scent. They don't like the smell of lavender," Carter whispered.

The aggressive snakes lunged at them again. Both boys grabbed the lavender flowers from their pockets and held them toward the horned vipers. As each snake came closer, they were repelled by the lavender scent.

The boys took a couple steps forward, and the horned vipers backed away.

"Eli, let's walk back to back. That way, we can hold the lavender out on all sides," Carter suggested.

They walked back to back in sync, slowly taking one step at a time. Then, with snakes all around them, the fragrance from the lavender flowers cleared a path for them to escape.

When they reached the end of the canyon, the snakes stopped at the opening. It was as if they couldn't leave. Finally, the horned serpents slithered up the side of the canyon back to their dens.

Carter took a deep breath, able to relax. "That was close."

"Too close," Eli said, shaking his head.

Chapter 13
On the Count of Three

Eli rechecked his watch. "We're running out of time. We have to be back by dinner."

"We're almost there. I can feel it. Let's race," Carter said, taking off.

Eli ran after his brother and quickly caught up. "Hey, don't run so far ahead. We need to stay together."

Carter and Eli chased each other as they ran across the rocky terrain.

"Tag, you're it!" Eli shouted back to Carter

as he passed and tapped him on the shoulder.

Instantly, Carter sped up to catch Eli. They chased each other, laughing, playing, and taking turns being it. Then, stepping back to avoid Carter tagging him, Eli tripped on a large rock and stumbled.

"WATCH OUT!" Carter screamed. "Don't move."

Eli turned around. "Whoa!" he trembled and slowly crept toward Carter.

They were standing next to a steep cliff. Distracted by their game, the boys hadn't noticed that they had reached the other side of the island. Carter peered over the edge while Eli stayed back, nervous about the great height. Below, the teal-blue sea appeared far away.

"Where do we go from here," Carter asked, feeling uneasy. "We've crossed the rocky terrain, but there's nowhere else to go. Maybe we went the wrong way."

"Let's look at the riddle," Eli suggested, grabbing the weathered paper from their waterproof bag.

Start where ancient civilizations collide
Past the island that moves with the tide
Pick a fragrant field, for protection it provides
Stop at the farthest rock as you have arrived
Cross the rocky terrain and then take a dive
Hold your breath and follow a friend inside.

"The riddle says *to take a dive*."

"What? We're supposed to jump off a cliff?" Carter cried. "It's too high. There must be another way down."

The boys searched the area for a path down to the water, but nothing was in sight.

Carter walked over to the edge again to see how far the jump was. "We've come this far. I guess we have to try."

"I don't know, Carter. This is dangerous. We could get badly hurt."

"But Eli, Seymour is right behind us. He's been following us the whole time," Carter urged. "What if he catches up to us and steals the map piece."

Eli knew his brother was right but wasn't

convinced. "What if the treasure isn't worth it?"

"Remember what the letter said," Carter continued. "We could all be at risk if the wrong person finds the Hidden World. We can't just stop."

"I know. You're right," Eli took a deep breath. "We were chosen to complete this quest. We have to try."

"We'll do it together," Carter said, holding his hand for Eli to take.

Slowly they walked to the edge. "We jump together on three," Eli said.

With a shaking voice, Carter looked up at his older brother and muttered, "R-r-ready?"

Eli nodded. "One, two, three, JUMP!" And the boys leapt off the cliff.

Chapter 14
Follow a Friend

SPLASH!

Eli opened his eyes underwater and found himself deep below the surface. In the darkness, his lungs burned for air. He fought his way through the current until he felt the sun's warmth on his face and could take a large breath in.

Feeling dazed from the fall, Eli floated on the waves for a few moments, wondering how long he had been underwater. Then he realized he was alone.

"CARTER!" Eli screamed. "CARTER, WHERE ARE YOU?"

Terrified, Eli kicked his feet to turn in a circle, searching in all directions. Calm waves surrounded him. He dove under the water, but

Carter was nowhere in sight.

Suddenly, Eli felt something touch his leg. "Carter!" he yelled, feeling relieved.

He swam below the surface to find his brother, but through the shadows, he saw a strange figure. Startled, Eli quickly resurfaced

and kicked to escape. Once at a safe distance, he dove underwater again to find Carter. This time, a pair of dark eyes were staring right at him.

"AHHH!" Eli screamed.

Then, the dark creature popped out of the water and sprayed Eli in the face. Using his arm, Eli wiped his eyes and got his first look at the stranger.

"A seal!" Eli said, surprised.

The seal dove down again and resurfaced just as quickly as before, but this time, he wasn't alone. Carter was resting over the seal's back.

Amazed by the sea animal, Eli grabbed his brother, turned him over, and patted his back. Carter began coughing and then opened his eyes.

Eli held Carter under the arms so his head stayed above water. "Are you okay?"

Carter blinked several times, confused about where he was. "I think so," he gasped between coughs.

The playful seal swam up to the boys and nudged Carter's arm.

"I think he's checking to see if you're alright," Eli said, smiling.

Carter rubbed his eyes and saw the seal. "Thank you. You saved my life."

The seal came in close, turned sharply, and slammed his tail into the water. The splash felt like a tidal wave.

Carter laughed. "I think he wants to play."

"He's swimming back," Eli replied.

The boys swam and splashed around with their new friend. Eli practiced diving while Carter tried to copy how the seal swam by keeping his arms against his sides and moving his body up and down. After some time, they made their way toward land.

For the first time, Eli noticed a tall, thin rectangular opening on the island. The rock face jutted out, keeping the entrance to a cave well hidden. From most angles, the gap would be difficult to see from a boat.

As the trio neared the entrance, the seal

gently nudged them inside. Then, staring in awe, Carter and Eli whispered, "Hold your breath and follow a friend inside."

Chapter 15
The Missing Map

Carter entered the cave and hesitated. He peered ahead, noticing the fading sunlight, and trembled.

Eli saw the expression on Carter's face, knowing how afraid his little brother was of the dark. "It will be okay, Carter, we have our flashlights, and we'll stick together."

The three friends ventured inside the cave. It was as black as night until Eli and Carter clicked on their lights. Once their eyes adjusted to the glow, several tunnels shaped by large rock formations appeared. The seal moved ahead, guiding them through one of the twisty water paths. As they swam farther, the water became more and more shallow. Soon, Carter and Eli were able to touch the bottom.

"Harp! Harp! Harp!" the seal barked, pulling himself out of the water onto a beach.

"I wonder if he's trying to lead us to the map piece," Carter called back, swimming faster.

Carter and Eli reached the shore. The small and narrow cove was surrounded by towering rock walls on three sides. Instead of sand, the beach was made up of soft black pebbles. They reminded Eli of his polished rock collection back home.

The boys waded out of the water and found the stones slippery to walk on. With each step, the rocks shifted, and they lost their balance.

"Where should we start?" Eli asked.

Carter began digging in the pebbles. "I don't know. It could be anywhere."

"Harp! Harp! Harp!" The seal was trying to

get their attention again. Finally, he wiggled his way up the back of the beach.

"What are you trying to show us?" Eli asked, feeling the smooth side of the rock wall with his hands. "Is it hidden in the wall?"

"Do you see anything?" Carter asked, walking over to Eli with the flashlight.

Moving their hands across the rocks, the boys felt for rough edges or cracks. As Eli crouched down low, the seal barked again.

"He's directing us to the map," Carter said.

Eli continued searching with the help of their new friend when suddenly, he felt something rough. "Carter, shine your light over here," Eli called.

Carter rushed over. The light exposed a small crack in the rock face. Using his hand, Eli brushed away the dirt and uncovered a small stone that was edged into the rock. He forced his fingers into the narrow gap and pulled. "It's stuck," Eli explained. "We're going to have to dig it out."

Carter reached into his pocket for his Swiss

Army knife. "We can use the small knife to chisel the rock and make the cracks bigger."

"Good idea," Eli said.

While Eli sat patiently next to the seal, Carter picked away at the rock. Then, after some time, Carter carved enough rock to easily slip his fingers around the stone. He pulled as hard as he could, and the rock wiggled. "It's working," Carter said excitedly, "but I need your help."

Eli joined Carter. Together they gripped the rock and tugged at the stone. Finally, the rock came loose, and the boys fell backward onto the black pebbles.

Eli turned the flat stone over and yelled, "This is it. The symbol from great-grandma Liv's letter is on the back."

Carter's eyes widened with surprise. He crawled over to the small hole in the wall.

Glancing inside, Carter grabbed two pieces of weathered paper and passed the next riddle to Eli. "We found it! We're one step closer to finding the Hidden World," Carter cheered, holding the second map piece.

"Harp! Harp! Harp!" the seal barked excitedly, leaning over their shoulders to see their discovery.

Eli rechecked his watch. "Carter, it's almost dinner time. We have to get going."

He handed Carter the waterproof bag to put the papers in and walked back to the water.

"Wait, let's take a few stones as a souvenir," Carter suggested, picking up a handful of black pebbles and putting them in the bag.

Eli smiled at the seal. "Are you coming?" he asked, and the seal squirmed back to the water.

They followed the seal out of the cave, back into the daylight. Then, with their eyes squinting from the bright sun, the boys spotted the giant cliff.

"How are we going to get back up there?" Carter asked. "There's no way to climb it."

Eli looked around to see if there was another way up, but he couldn't see a different way.

"Harp! Harp! Harp!" the seal barked, then splashed the boys as he swam away.

The boys followed the seal as he guided them around the corner of the island.

"He must know another way," Eli said, swimming faster to keep up.

Chapter 16
Daring Deception

"WAIT!" Carter called after Eli and the seal.

Exhausted from the long swim, Carter started to slow down. Finally, he stopped and floated on his back to catch his breath, unable to keep up anymore.

Eli and the seal swam back to check on him. "Are you okay?"

"I need a break," Carter replied.

The seal nudged him again, encouraging Carter to keep swimming.

"I'm sorry, buddy. I'm not sure how much farther I can go," Carter said, petting the seal.

The seal went over to Eli, and he grabbed the floating waterproof bag by the strap.

"No, don't take that," Eli cried, trying to get it back.

Using his nose, the seal tossed the bag to Carter.

"Why didn't I think of that," Eli said, laughing. "Carter, hold on to the bag to help you float."

Relieved, Carter hugged the round bag and rested. Then, the seal swam up, took the strap in his mouth, and began to swim, pulling Carter behind him.

"He's helping you, Carter," Eli shouted, amazed by the seal again. "Kick your feet."

Carter began kicking, and the seal pulled him along. Soon, they saw their sailboat. They had gone around the whole island.

They reached the boat, and it was time to say goodbye to their friend.

Tears filled Carter's eyes. "Thank you for

everything. I will miss you."

Both boys gave the seal a big hug and then climbed into their boat. The seal jumped out of the water several times, waving his flippers as if to say goodbye. As the boys raised the sails, the seal followed beside the boat for a few moments and then disappeared into the sea.

"Carter, let the jib out. We have to go full speed back to make it in time," Eli shouted.

Carter ran to the bow of the boat and organized the sail. Within minutes, both sails were up, and they were on their way home.

As Carter and Eli entered the narrow channel near Brac island, they heard a loud sound. Coming up fast behind them was a speedboat.

"That boat is too close," Eli shouted. "He's going to hit us."

The faster boat caught up to them quickly, swerving next to them, nearly hitting the side of their sailboat. The giant wave from the speedboat's wake crashed into their boat, causing Carter and Eli to stumble.

Confused, the boys stood up and looked around for the speedboat. It was coming right for them again.

"Why is that boat coming so close to us?" Carter cried, holding on to the mast to keep his balance.

"I don't know," Eli replied.

The speedboat headed straight for their boat, the engine revving at full speed. Eli saw the driver when the boat passed them, nearly hitting them once more.

"Seymour!" Eli shouted.

All the colour drained from Carter's face. He was terrified. "What are we going to do? We can't outrun him in a sailboat."

Seymour came at them again. His small eyes narrowed in on them, focused on his plan. "You can't escape me. Give up the map," he yelled.

"Never!" Eli shouted.

Seymour turned his boat in front of them, creating another large wave, causing the sailboat to tilt. Eli fell to the ground hitting his head on the deck.

"Are you hurt?" Carter asked, rushing to help Eli.

"I'm alright." Eli stood up, rubbing a small bump on the back of his head. "But you're right. We can't outrun a speedboat," Eli agreed. "We'll have to outsmart him instead."

Eli thought for a minute, trying to figure out a plan. Then out of the corner of his eye, he saw a bright red buoy marking a shallow area in the water.

"Look over there, Carter. If we head toward the shore, Seymour will get caught on the rocks," Eli explained, pointing to the right. "Steer the boat near the red buoy."

Carter took hold of the tiller and turned the boat. Seymour noticed the boys changing course and followed them. He headed straight for their boat. Carter navigated the sailboat next to the buoy, blocking it from Seymour's view.

As he came closer, Seymour's eyes bulged in terror. For the first time, he saw a flash of red. He quickly swerved around the buoy to miss it.

CRASH!

The speedboat smashed into the rocks in the shallow area. Water poured in from a massive hole in the bow of the boat.

Furious, Seymour stood up, waving his fists in the air. "I'll get you next time. That treasure is mine."

Feeling victorious, Carter and Eli quickly changed course away from the crash and sailed toward Split.

Once at a safe distance, Carter wondered what Seymour might do if he ever caught up to them. He glanced over at Eli, thankful that his brother was able to find a way to escape Seymour today but afraid their luck might not be as good the next time.

Chapter 17
The Next Adventure

The sun was setting as Carter and Eli walked into the apartment. Exhausted from the day's events, they dragged themselves to the dinner table where their parents sat.

"You guys were gone a long time," their dad said. "Did you spend the whole day at the palace?"

"No, we did a bit of exploring," Eli said, looking over to his brother, and Carter giggled.

"Well, I would guess so. You two are filthy,"

their mom said, eyeing their dirty clothes and scraped knees. "You can have a quick dinner and then into the bath."

After getting ready for bed, their parents tucked them in and turned off the light. Once they could no longer hear footsteps outside their bedroom door, Eli rolled over and grabbed the waterproof bag from the floor. He opened the bag and took out the papers.

Finally, they were going to be able to read the next riddle. Barely able to contain their excitement, they looked at each other and smiled. Where were they headed next?

> The next country that you seek
> Has an ancient past
> Thriving on a riverbank
> And a life that lasts and lasts.

www.ingramcontent.com/pod-product-compliance
Lightning Source LLC
LaVergne TN
LVHW021943060526
838200LV00042B/1904